UNITED STATES BY REGION

People and Places of the
NORTHEAST
by John Micklos, Jr.

Consultant:
Dr. David Lanegran
John S. Holl Professor of Geography
Macalester College
St. Paul, Minnesota

CAPSTONE PRESS
a capstone imprint

Fact Finders Books are published by Capstone Press,
1710 Roe Crest Drive, North Mankato, Minnesota 56003
www.mycapstone.com

Copyright © 2017 by Capstone Press, a Capstone imprint. All rights reserved. No part of this publication may be reproduced in whole or in part, or stored in a retrieval system, or transmitted in any form or by any means, electronic, mechanical, photocopying, recording, or otherwise, without written permission of the publisher.

Library of Congress Cataloging-in-Publication Data
Names: Micklos, John, author.
Title: People and places of the Northeast / by John Micklos, Jr.
Description: North Mankato, Minnesota : Capstone Press, [2017] | Includes bibliographical references and index.
Identifiers: LCCN 2016008943 | ISBN 9781515724445 (library binding) | ISBN 9781515724490 (pbk.) | ISBN 9781515724544 (ebook : .pdf)
Subjects: LCSH: Northeastern States—Juvenile literature.
Classification: LCC F4.3 .M53 2017 | DDC 974—dc23
LC record available at http://lccn.loc.gov/2016008943

Editorial Credits
Angie Kaelberer, editor; Cynthia Della-Rovere, designer; Svetlana Zhurkin, media researcher; Laura Manthe, production specialist

Photo Credits
Library of Congress, 12; NASA, 21; Newscom: akg-images, 10–11; North Wind Picture Archives, 8–9, 9; Shutterstock: Benjamin Sullivan, 16, Christian Delbert, 23, Doug Lemke, cover (top), Francois Roux, 17, Jaminnbenji, 15, kan_khampanya, 6, Liviu Toader, 29, Nagel Photography, 22, Noel Moore, cover (bottom), Olivier Le Queinec, 25, RomanSlavik, 20, Samuel Borges Photography, 27, sianc, 19; SuperStock: ClassicStock, 13

Design and Map Elements by Shutterstock

Table of Contents

Introduction 4

Chapter 1: People and History 8

Chapter 2: Land and Climate 14

Chapter 3: Daily Life and Economy . . 20

Chapter 4: Culture and Recreation . . . 26

Glossary *30*

Read More *31*

Internet Sites *31*

Index *32*

Introduction

The Northeast region of the United States is famous for its large, busy cities. Many cities are filled with tall skyscrapers. But the region is also the home of white-capped mountains, thick forests, and clear lakes.

The Northeast is the smallest U.S. region in land size. It stretches about 750 miles (1,207 kilometers) from the northern tip of Maine to the southern borders of Pennsylvania and New Jersey. It includes the states of New York, New Jersey, and Pennsylvania. It also includes the New England states of Maine, New Hampshire, Vermont, Massachusetts, Rhode Island, and Connecticut.

Some areas of the Northeast are packed with people. Six of the nine states are among the nation's top 10 in **population density**. But Maine is the least densely populated state east of the Mississippi River.

population density: the number of people living within a certain area, such as per square mile

The Northeast was the birthplace of the United States. Each of its states was important in forming the country we know today.

The Northeast Region by Rank

Let's see how the states in the Northeast compare to each other. This chart includes each state in the Northeast and ranks it by population and area. Also included are each state's capital and nickname. Some of the nicknames make sense for the state. Some may require a little more research to find out why that state earned the nickname.

Vermont's forest-filled mountains helped earn the state its nickname.

State	Population	Rank	Square Miles	Rank	Capital	Nickname
Connecticut	3,596,677	29	5,544	48	Hartford	Constitution State
Maine	1,330,089	41	35,387	39	Augusta	Pine Tree State
Massachusetts	6,745,408	14	10,555	43	Boston	Bay State
New Hampshire	1,326,813	42	9,351	45	Concord	Granite State
New Jersey	8,938,175	11	8,722	46	Trenton	Garden State
New York	19,746,227	4	54,475	27	Albany	Empire State
Pennsylvania	12,787,209	6	46,058	33	Harrisburg	Keystone State
Rhode Island	1,055,173	43	1,545	50	Providence	Ocean State
Vermont	626,630	50	9,615	44	Montpelier	Green Mountain State

Chapter 1

People and History

American Indians lived in the Northeast region for thousands of years before Europeans arrived. Dozens of tribes traveled through the forests and fields. They hunted, fished, and grew crops. Tribes included the Lenni Lenape, Abenaki, Shawnee, and Iroquois **League**.

Some of the nation's earliest European settlements were in the Northeast. The Pilgrims settled in Plymouth, Massachusetts, in 1620. In 1626 Peter Minuit started a settlement where Manhattan is now. He bought the entire island from local Indians for goods worth a small amount of money. His purchase was one of the biggest bargains in history.

league: a group or organization

As more settlers arrived, American Indians were pushed from their lands. Europeans also brought deadly diseases, such as measles and smallpox. Thousands of Indians died from these and other diseases.

American Indians built longhouses like these in what is now Manhattan.

Tisquantum

Tisquantum of the Patuxet tribe helped the Pilgrims survive in the New World. Tisquantum had been kidnapped by English explorers years earlier and taken to Europe. He learned to speak English there. He eventually returned to his home area. He taught the Pilgrims to plant corn. He also served as an interpreter and helped them make treaties with nearby tribes.

Historical Importance

The Northeast has played a major role throughout our nation's history. Most battles of the Revolutionary War (1775–1783) were fought in the region. In Colonial times Boston led the protest against British taxes. In 1776 Philadelphia hosted the signing of the Declaration of Independence as the colonies broke away from British rule. The city also served as the nation's capital before it was moved to Washington, D.C.

In the 1800s the issue of slavery divided the nation. By 1804 all northern states had outlawed slavery. They believed southern states should do the same. The struggle over slavery led to 11 southern states **seceding** from the Union. They formed the Confederate States of America. The Union and the Confederacy then fought the bloody Civil War (1861–1865).

secede: to formally withdraw from a group or organization, often to form another group

On July 4, 1776, the Declaration of Independence was signed. This document stated that the 13 colonies were no longer under British rule.

After the Union won the Civil War, many former slaves moved to northeastern cities seeking better education and jobs. Meanwhile immigrants from all over the world settled in the Northeast. The region grew throughout most of the 1900s. People moved from the crowded cities into nearby **suburbs**.

The Northeast led the growth of U.S. industry in the 1800s and 1900s. Pennsylvania became a center for the steel industry. New York City had many **finance** companies. The region remains a national leader in many economic areas today.

Pittsburgh, Pennsylvania, was home to many steel mills in the early 1900s.

suburb: a town that's very close to a large city

finance: management and use of money by businesses, banks, and governments

Ellis Island

Between 1892 and 1954, more than 12 million immigrants passed through Ellis Island in Upper New York Bay. Most came from Europe. The Statue of Liberty in New York Harbor was often their first sight of their new country. Today this island is the home of the Ellis Island Museum of Immigration.

Chapter 2

Land and Climate

Several major mountain ranges are located in the Northeast. These include the Allegheny, Blue Ridge, Pocono, Catskill, Berkshire, Adirondack, and White Mountains. These mountains are all part of the Appalachian Mountain range. It stretches from Alabama into Canada. The 2,185-mile (3,516-km) Appalachian Trail goes through all northeastern states except Rhode Island. The trail begins in Georgia and ends at Mount Katahdin in Maine.

Other areas are low and flat. New Jersey and Rhode Island are among the states with the lowest overall elevation. Rhode Island's highest point is only 812 feet (247 meters).

This part of the Appalachian Trail is in the White Mountains Franconia Ridge. It's found in New Hampshire.

FACT

Over the years more than 15,000 people have hiked the entire Appalachian Trail. Some do it all at once. Others do it one section at a time. Some people take years to complete the entire trail.

Major rivers flow through the region too. These include the Hudson, Susquehanna, Connecticut, and Delaware. Large lakes include two of the Great Lakes, Lake Erie and Lake Ontario. Other famous lakes are the Finger Lakes and Lake Champlain in New York. The region's most famous water landmark is Niagara Falls. These three huge waterfalls stretch across the border between New York and Canada.

Six of the nine Northeast states touch the Atlantic Ocean. Maine's coastline is rocky and rugged. Its chilly ocean waters peak at 62 degrees Fahrenheit (17 degrees Celsius) in the summer. New Jersey has flat, sandy beaches. The average water temperature in Cape May, New Jersey, hits 74°F (23°C) in July and August.

Visitors to Portland Head Light in Maine can see a beautiful and historic lighthouse. The lighthouse was built in 1791 under the direction of George Washington.

Temperature and Precipitation

Upper northeastern states have cold climates. The temperature fell to −19 °F (−28°C) in January 2015 in northern Maine. States such as Pennsylvania and New Jersey are warmer. Philadelphia has an average high temperature from 39°F (4°C) in January to 85°F (29°C) in July.

Some parts of northern New York receive more than 100 inches (254 centimeters) of snow each year. That's more than 8 feet (2.5 m)! Maine, Vermont, and New Hampshire also get lots of snow. The states farther south get far less. Cape May in southern New Jersey has about 15 inches (38 cm) of snow each winter.

A snowy day can make Central Park in New York City seem like a quiet place.

Animals and Plants

The Northeast is home to a wide variety of animals and plants. Whales glide through the ocean waters near the coasts of Massachusetts and Long Island, New York. Geese and other birds **migrate** over the region each fall as they fly south for the winter. They pass through again in the spring as they return north.

Maine is known for lobsters and moose. People in the Northeast often trap lobsters. Trapping lobsters is hard work. Lobster boats sail around jagged rocks in freezing ocean water. Lobster catchers place dead fish or other bait in their lobster traps. Then they drop the traps to the ocean floor with ropes. Hungry lobsters enter the traps looking for food. The catchers check their traps for lobsters every day or two.

migrate: to move from one area to another

FACT

Forests cover nearly 90 percent of Maine. That's the highest percentage of any state!

Major tree types include cedar, oak, pine, and maple. New England states produce more than half of the nation's maple syrup. Vermont produces 40 percent of the nation's total.

This man is tapping a maple tree. The sap that comes out of the tap will be used later to make syrup.

Chapter 3
Daily Life and Economy

Several of the nation's largest and most important cities are in the Northeast. New York City is by far the nation's largest city. Nicknamed "The Big Apple," it's home to more than 8 million people. One and a half million people live in Philadelphia. Other major cities in the region include Boston, Massachusetts; Pittsburgh, Pennsylvania; Providence, Rhode Island; Newark, New Jersey; Hartford, Connecticut; and Buffalo and Syracuse in New York.

New York City has quite a breathtaking skyline from the Brooklyn Bridge.

Endless Cities

Much of the Northeast is crowded with people. The area between Washington, D.C., and Boston is called a **megalopolis**. The cities and suburbs form what nearly amounts to one massive city. That area includes 17 percent of the nation's people clustered on 2 percent of its land area. New Jersey has the highest population density of any state. About 94 percent of New Jersey residents live in cities.

The megalopolis is lit up from space.

FACT

The Brooklyn Bridge, completed in 1883, is one of the world's most famous bridges. It spans the East River, connecting the **boroughs** of Brooklyn and Manhattan.

megalopolis: an area where cities and suburbs have merged to the point of nearly being one giant city

boroughs: the five divisions of New York City, each of which is also a county

Although known for its big cities, the Northeast also has many interesting small towns. *Smithsonian* magazine named Nantucket, Massachusetts; Stowe, Vermont; and Cooperstown, New York, among the 20 best U.S. small towns to visit. Nantucket is known for its wharf and lighthouses, while Stowe is famous for its ski resorts. Cooperstown is home to the National Baseball Hall of Fame and Museum.

Many famous baseball players are honored at the National Baseball Hall of Fame and Museum.

A major road system crisscrosses the Northeast. The longest highway is I-95. This road stretches nearly 2,000 miles (3,200 km) from Maine to Florida. It passes through every Northeast state except Vermont.

Economy

The Northeast is famous for manufacturing. It was the first region in the country to develop heavy industry in the 1800s. Pennsylvania became a center for coal mining and steel manufacturing in the 1900s. Both of those industries are less important today. Many service and technology jobs have replaced the manufacturing jobs. However, Pennsylvania and New York still rank among the top 10 states in manufacturing jobs.

Fishing is also important in coastal states. New Bedford, Massachusetts, has long ranked as a top commercial fishing port. In 2012, 143 million pounds (65 million kilograms) of seafood were brought ashore. More than three out of every four lobsters caught in the nation comes from Maine. The lobster industry added about $1.7 billion to Maine's economy in 2012.

Many fishing boats can be found in New Bedford Harbor in Massachusetts.

The Northeast states have active farming and dairy industries. The region produces many crops. Maine is the top producer of potatoes in the eastern United States. Massachusetts and New Jersey rank among the top five states in cranberry production. New Jersey ranks fifth for blueberries. New York ranks second in apple production.

The Northeast is also a major financial center. The New York Stock Exchange is the world's largest **stock market**. The U.S. Mint in Philadelphia produces an amazing 13.5 billion coins every year. Many insurance companies are based in Connecticut.

New York City is an entertainment and tourism capital too. People come to the city's theater district to see plays and shows. This is centered on Broadway Street. The terrorist attack of September 11, 2001, hurt tourism in New York for many years. So did the recession from 2007 through 2009. But tourism has bounced back in recent years.

stock market: a place where stocks are bought and sold

These farmers are harvesting cranberries in a bog in New Jersey.

Chapter 4
Culture and Recreation

The Northeast region is rich in American historical sites. Visit Pennsylvania to see the Liberty Bell, Valley Forge, and the Gettysburg Battlefield. Then travel to Boston to see the Bunker Hill Monument and to visit the Old North Church. Paul Revere ordered lanterns to be hung at the church to warn Colonial soldiers that British troops were leaving Boston in April 1775. New Jersey is also the site of several Revolutionary War battlefields, including Monmouth and Trenton.

The Northeast's major cities are cultural centers for museums, plays, and concerts. New York City is the home of Carnegie Hall, the Metropolitan Opera, the Metropolitan Museum of Art, and the American Museum of Natural History. The Boston Children's Museum is the second-oldest children's museum in the world. Boston also offers the John F. Kennedy Presidential Library and Museum and the Boston Tea Party Ships and Museum. Philadelphia's Museum of Art is a world-class museum. People can visit it to see large collections of art from around the world.

Several of the nation's top professional sports teams call the Northeast home. The New York Yankees have won more World Series titles than any other baseball team. The Boston Celtics have won the most NBA titles. The Pittsburgh Steelers have won the most Super Bowl rings.

Visitors to Philadelphia's Museum of Art can race up the outdoor steps, just as the character Rocky Balboa did in the *Rocky* movies.

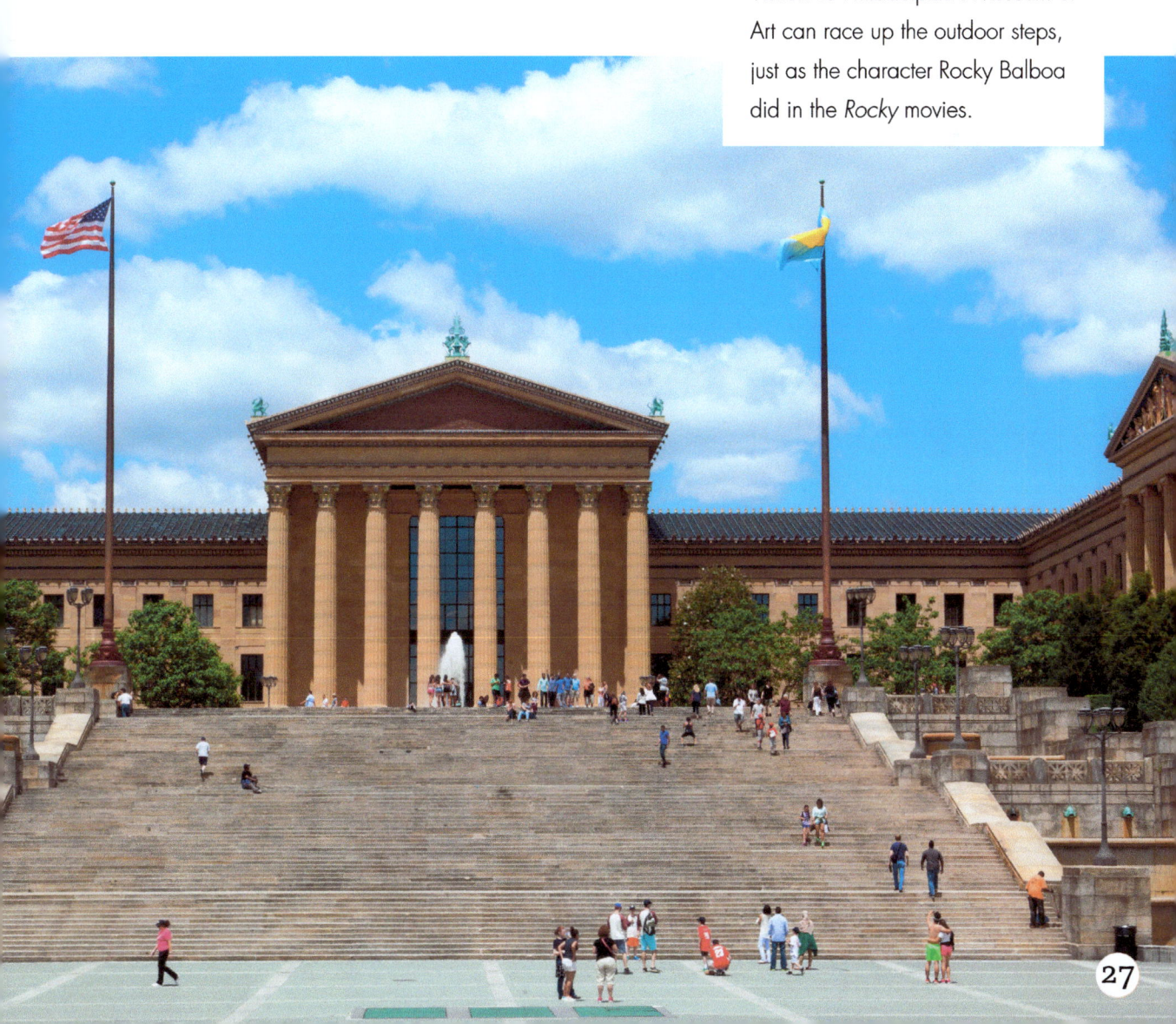

A Rich Heritage

The Northeast has a rich **ethnic** heritage from the millions of immigrants who came to the region. Massachusetts has a large number of people of Irish heritage. New York is home to more Puerto Ricans than any other place outside of Puerto Rico. Many Portuguese immigrants live in Rhode Island and southeastern Massachusetts. These ethnic groups and many others brought their food, music, and culture to the region.

People enjoy outdoor activities during all four seasons in the Northeast. Skiers and snowboarders carve the powdered slopes at resorts on many of the region's mountains. Visitors also gather on beaches and boardwalks along the Atlantic Ocean. Others come to the Northeast each autumn to see the fall **foliage**. The season lasts from late September to mid-October.

> **ethnic:** having to do with a group of people sharing the same language, traditions, and religion
>
> **foliage:** leaves of trees or plants

The region truly offers something for everyone. From giant cities to small suburbs to nearly deserted forests and sandy beaches, the Northeast has it all.

These men are playing their bagpipes during a St. Patrick's Day Parade in Boston, Massachusetts.

Glossary

boroughs (BUHR-ohs)—the five divisions of New York City, each of which is also a county

ethnic (ETH-nik)—having to do with a group of people sharing the same language, traditions, and religion

finance (FYE-nanss)—management and use of money by businesses, banks, and governments

foliage (FOH-lee-ij)—leaves of trees or plants

league (LEEG)—a group or organization

megalopolis (meh-guh-LAH-puh-luhss)—an area where cities and suburbs have merged to the point of nearly being one giant city

migrate (MYE-grate)—to move from one area to another

population density (pop-yuh-LAY-shuhn DEN-si-tee)—the number of people living within a certain area, such as a square mile

secede (si-SEED)—to formally withdraw from a group or organization, often to form another group

stock market (STOK MAHR-kit)—a place where stocks are bought and sold

suburb (SUH-buhrb)—a town that's very close to a large city

Read More

Felix, Rebecca. *The Northeast.* Mankato, Minn: Child's World, 2013.

Linde, Barbara M. *Native Peoples of the Northeast.* Native Peoples of North America. New York: Gareth Stevens Publishing, 2017.

Peppas, Lynn. *What's in the Northeast?* All Around the U.S. New York: Crabtree Publishing Company, 2012.

Rau, Dana Meachen. *The Northeast.* A True Book. New York: Children's Press, 2012.

Internet Sites

FactHound offers a safe, fun way to find Internet sites related to this book. All of the sites on FactHound have been researched by our staff.

Here's all you do:

Visit www.facthound.com

Type in this code: 9781515724445

Check out projects, games and lots more at
www.capstonekids.com

Index

American Indians, 8–9
    Tisquantum, 9

animals, 18

Appalachian Trail, 14, 15

Atlantic Ocean, 16, 28

cities, 4, 12, 20–22, 26, 29
    Boston, 7, 10, 20, 21, 26, 27, 29
    New York City, 12, 20, 24, 26
    Philadelphia, 10, 17, 20, 24, 26

Civil War, 10, 12

climate, 17
    snow, 17,
    temperatures, 16, 17

Ellis Island, 13

farming, 24

fishing, 8, 18, 23

forests, 4, 8, 19, 29

jobs, 12, 23

manufacturing, 23

mining, 23

Minuit, Peter, 8

mountains, 4, 14, 28

museums, 13, 22, 26

Pilgrims, 8, 9

plants, 18, 19

Revere, Paul, 26

Revolutionary War, 10, 26
    Declaration of Independence, 10

slavery, 10, 12

sports teams, 27

stock market, 24

tourism, 24